The Civil War's African-American Soldiers Through Primary Sources

Carin T. Ford

Enslow Publishers, Inc.
40 Industrial Road
Box 398
Berkeley Heights, NJ 07922
USA

http://www.enslow.com

Original edition published as *African-American Soldiers in the Civil War: Fighting for Freedom* in 2004.

Library of Congress Cataloging-in-Publication Data

Ford, Carin T.
  [African-American soldiers in the Civil War]
  The Civil War's African-American soldiers through primary sources / Carin T. Ford.
      pages cm. — (The Civil War through primary sources)
  "Original edition published as African-American Soldiers in the Civil War: Fighting for Freedom in 2004."
  Includes bibliographical references and index.
  Summary: "Examines African-American soldiers during the Civil War, including the reasons for African Americans
to fight, the all-black regiments, the treatment of African Americans, and the important role they played in the Union
victory"—Provided by publisher.
  ISBN 978-0-7660-4125-7
  1. United States—History—Civil War, 1861–1865—Participation, African American—Juvenile literature. 2. African
American soldiers—History—19th century—Juvenile literature. [1. African American soldiers—History—19th century.
2. United States—History—Civil War, 1861–1865—Participation, African American. 3. Race relations—History.] I.
Title.
  E540.N3F675 2013
  973.7'415—dc23
                                        2012031282
Future editions:
Paperback ISBN: 978-1-4644-0183-1
EPUB ISBN: 978-1-4645-1096-0
Single-User PDF ISBN: 978-1-4646-1096-7
Multi-User PDF ISBN: 978-0-7660-5725-8

Printed in China

012013 Leo Paper Group, Heshan City, Guangdong, China

10 9 8 7 6 5 4 3 2 1

To Our Readers: We have done our best to make sure all Internet addresses in this book were active and appropriate when we went to press. However, the author and the publisher have no control over and assume no liability for the material available on those Internet sites or on other Web sites they may link to. Any comments or suggestions can be sent by e-mail to comments@enslow.com or to the address on the back cover.

Illustration Credits: Enslow Publishers, Inc., p. 9; George F. Landegger Collection of District of Columbia Photographs in Carol M. Highsmith's America, Library of Congress Prints and Photographs, pp. 28–29; Library of Congress Prints and Photographs, pp. 1, 2–3, 4–5, 8, 10, 12, 13, 14, 16, 19, 22, 24, 26, 27, 32, 34, 36, 38, 41; National Archives and Records Administration, pp. 17, 21, 40.

Cover Illustration: Library of Congress Prints and Photographs (Two unidentified African-American Union soldiers).

CONTENTS

★

LOOK FOR THIS SYMBOL **PRIMARY SOURCE** TO FIND THE PRIMARY SOURCES THROUGHOUT THIS BOOK.

In this illustration, the Fifty-fourth Massachusetts Regiment storms Fort Wagner in July 1863. The Fifty-fourth regiment was one of the first all-black units fighting in the Civil War.

CHAPTER 1

---★---

A NEW COUNTRY

Six hundred Union soldiers raced toward Fort Wagner in South Carolina. The men were wet, tired, and hungry. It was July 1863, and the Fifty-fourth Massachusetts Regiment was one of the first units of African-American soldiers fighting in the Civil War. One soldier carried the Union flag, showing that the men were fighting for the North. Colonel Robert Gould Shaw had told his soldiers to "take the fort or die there."[1] The men promised to try. Yet, inside the fort, nearly three times as many Confederate soldiers were waiting with guns and cannons.

Bullets flew, and the Union soldiers fell, one after another. The soldier holding the Union flag was shot. Quickly, Sergeant

William H. Carney reached out and grabbed the flag. As the regiment was ordered back to camp, Carney ran through a storm of bullets. He was shot in the head, chest, arm, and leg—but he did not let go of the flag.

"The old flag never touched the ground," Carney said proudly when he was safely back at camp with his unit.[2]

The charge on Fort Wagner was a defeat for the North. The regiment lost almost half its men, including Colonel Robert Shaw. But the soldiers of the Fifty-fourth did not feel defeated. They had shown their courage. They had proved that black men could be soldiers.

*****

When the Civil War broke out in April 1861, very few people thought African Americans should be allowed to fight. It was called a white man's war, meaning it was up to whites to serve in the army and navy.[3] Yet the war had everything to do with black Americans.

There had been slavery in the United States for nearly 250 years. It had begun when a Dutch ship brought twenty African

Who's Who in the Civil War

★ The North was also known as the Union, or the United States. The people there were often called Yankees.

★ The South was called the Confederate States, or the Confederacy. During the war, Southerners were also called Rebels or Johnny Reb.

slaves to Virginia in 1619. By the outbreak of the Civil War, there were close to 4 million slaves in the country. These people had no rights. They were bought and sold like property. Many slaves were torn away from their families, beaten, whipped, and half-starved.

Most slaves lived in the South. Tobacco, rice, sugarcane, and cotton grew well there. The slaves worked from sunrise to sunset planting, plowing, and harvesting the crops. After the cotton gin was invented in 1793, the demand for slaves skyrocketed. The cotton gin was a machine that removed the seeds from the cotton. Fifty times more cotton could be cleaned each day—and farmers could make even more money selling cotton. On their huge plantations, Southern farmers used slaves to produce nearly two-thirds of all the cotton grown in the world.

A group of slaves stands for a portrait on Smith's Plantation in Beaufort, South Carolina, in 1862. Southern plantation owners claimed that they needed slaves to grow their cotton or the thriving industry in the South would collapse.

People in the United States had different opinions about slavery. Most Southerners believed they needed slaves to grow cotton. In the North, the businesses and small farms did not depend on slave labor. Many Northerners began to say that it was wrong for one person to own another person.

A New Country

In November 1860, Abraham Lincoln was elected president. By then, one out of every seven Americans was a slave.[4] Lincoln had often spoken out against slavery. As president, would he put an end to it?

People in the South were worried. They did not think the government in Washington, D.C., had the right to tell them what to do about slavery. Southerners said each state should be able to decide for itself.

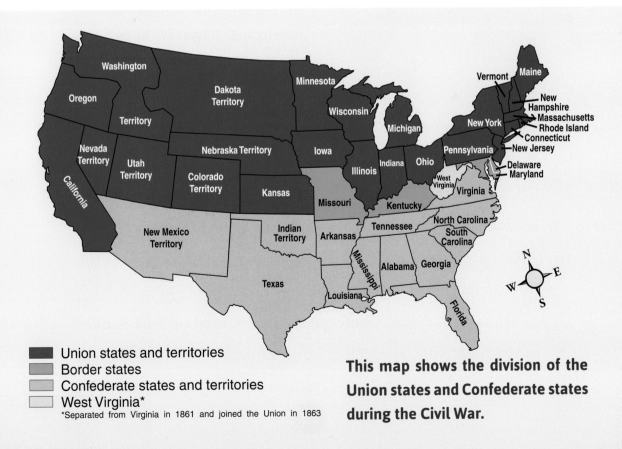

Union states and territories
Border states
Confederate states and territories
West Virginia*
*Separated from Virginia in 1861 and joined the Union in 1863

This map shows the division of the Union states and Confederate states during the Civil War.

Abraham Lincoln sits for a portrait on August 13, 1860. Although President Lincoln was outspoken against slavery, his initial reason for fighting the Civil War was to reunite the nation. African Americans, however, hoped the war would end slavery.

South Carolina seceded—or broke away—from the rest of the country in December 1860. Soon, six more Southern states followed: Mississippi, Florida, Alabama, Georgia, Louisiana, and Texas. Together, they formed a new country. They called it the Confederate States of America.

On April 12, 1861, Confederate soldiers fired on Fort Sumter in South Carolina. The United States soldiers surrendered the fort to the Confederates. The North and the South were at war. After that, four more slave states joined the Confederacy: Virginia, Arkansas, Tennessee, and North Carolina.

President Lincoln called for 75,000 volunteers to serve in the Union army and fight for the United States of America. He said he would not allow the nation to be split in two. The Civil War began as a fight to put the country back together. But African Americans hoped that a war between North and South would also put an end to slavery—and they wanted to take part in it.

Frederick Douglass was an ex-slave who became famous as a speaker and writer against slavery. He told African-American men and women to fight for their freedom. "I urge you to fly to arms," Douglass said. "This is your golden opportunity."[5]

Still, the U.S. War Department continued to turn away African Americans. Many white Northerners thought slavery was wrong, but they did not think black people were equal to whites. They did not want to fight side by side with black soldiers.

Frederick Douglass, the famous speaker and abolitionist, urged African Americans to fight for the Union cause.

Besides, most Northerners were certain the Civil War would be over in a few months. The Union had more factories, more guns, and more men than the Confederacy. The Union army said it did not need any help from African Americans.

"Let us do something . . . " Douglass urged the government. "We are ready and would go."[6] But when African Americans asked to help fight the war, the door was closed to them.

CHAPTER 2

★

THE WAY IS BARRED

A law from the late 1700s said that blacks could not fight in the United States Army. Yet, early in the Civil War, a few army officials tried to put together units of African-American soldiers. When the government would not supply them with guns, uniforms, or money, these units fell apart.

As the Civil War dragged on, many slaves escaped from their plantations and headed for Union army camps. Some Union officers sent the slaves back to their masters. However, often slaves were allowed to stay with the soldiers. They were called "contraband of war." This meant they were like goods taken from the enemy. Now they belonged to the North.

Escaped slaves who made their way to Union army camps and stayed with the soldiers were called contrabands. This photo taken on May 14, 1862, shows a group of contrabands outside a house in Cumberland Landing, Virginia.

The contrabands helped in any way they could. Men drove wagons, dug trenches for the soldiers, and worked as cooks and servants. Women did laundry, sewing, housekeeping, and nursing. Some were spies and scouts.

It was clear by the middle of 1862 that the war was not going to end quickly. More than twenty battles had been fought. The number of wounded and dead soldiers was growing. At the same

One Contraband's Story

Mary Ann Cox was a slave on a cotton plantation. Her first husband had been sold to another slave owner, and her second husband had died. In July 1863, Mary Ann ran away with her son, Everett. They joined a contraband camp in Tennessee. When Everett joined the Union army, Mary Ann traveled with the regiment as a washerwoman. After a fierce battle in Mississippi, Mary Ann waited for her son to return to camp. But Everett had been captured and later died in an Alabama prison.[1]

time, the number of white volunteer soldiers was dropping. The Union army needed more men.

In July 1862, the U.S. Congress gave President Lincoln the power to hire African-American soldiers.[2] He ordered Secretary of War Edwin Stanton to recruit black soldiers in the Sea Islands near South Carolina.

In this sketch that appeared in *Frank Leslie's Illustrated Newspaper* on March 18, 1865, contrabands accompany Union general William Tecumseh Sherman's troops on their march through Georgia.

By the President of the United States

A Proclamation.

Whereas, on the twenty-second day of September, in the year of our Lord one thousand eight hundred and sixty-two, a proclamation was issued by the President of the United States, containing, among other things, the following, to wit:

"That on the first day of January, in the "year of our Lord one thousand eight hundred "and sixty-three, all persons held as slaves within "any State or designated part of a State, the people "whereof shall then be in rebellion against the "United States, shall be then, thenceforward, and "forever free; and the Executive Government of the "United States, including the military and naval "authority thereof, will recognize and maintain "the freedom of such persons, and will do no act

President Lincoln issued the Emancipation Proclamation on January 1, 1863, granting all slaves in the rebel states their freedom. This is page one of the document.

Would Slaves Fight?

Most slaves in the South were loyal to their masters at the start of the war. But after the Emancipation Proclamation, many slaves learned that they had the chance to be free. Thousands of slaves ran away to join the Union army.[3]

On January 1, 1863, Lincoln issued the Emancipation Proclamation. It stated that all slaves in the rebelling states were now free.

Southerners did not set their slaves free just because Lincoln told them to. Lincoln had no power in the Confederate states. Still, the South lost many slaves as Union soldiers swept through to recruit men. The soldiers promised freedom to any male slave who joined the Union army.

The Emancipation Proclamation changed the reason for the Civil War. The war was no longer just about putting the country back together. Now soldiers were also fighting to put an end to slavery.

CHAPTER 3

★

RECRUITMENT

Once African Americans learned that they could serve in the army and the navy, they quickly started signing up. One man in New Orleans said that he would "fight as long as I can. If only my boy may stand in the street equal to a white boy when the war is over."[1]

Many of the new soldiers came from the North, where African-American businessmen and ministers urged men to join. They gave speeches, held meetings, and handed out flyers. Black soldiers were also telling other African Americans to enlist. "Let us make a name for ourselves and race," said one soldier at a meeting in Nashville, Tennessee.[2]

Enlistment

So many black men enlisted that a separate department was formed to handle them. It was called the Bureau of Colored Troops.

From the start, Lincoln knew that there would have to be separate units for the African-American soldiers. White Northerners worried about giving guns to black men. Also, few white men wanted to fight alongside black soldiers.

Flyers calling for men to join the Union army had two separate messages: one for whites, the other for blacks. Black men were told to prove that they could be good soldiers. Whites were told that the army needed more men—and that was why blacks were being asked to join.

Nearly all the officers in charge of the black units were white. The public, and the army, had a hard enough time with the idea of African-American soldiers. Lincoln believed that they would never accept African-American officers.

TO COLORED MEN!

FREEDOM,

Protection, Pay, and a Call to Military Duty!

On the 1st day of January, 1863, the President of the United States proclaimed FREEDOM to over THREE MILLIONS OF SLAVES. This decree is to be enforced by all the power of the Nation. On the 21st of July last he issued the following order:

PROTECTION OF COLORED TROOPS.

"WAR DEPARTMENT, ADJUTANT GENERAL'S OFFICE,
Washington, July 21.

"General Order, No. 233.

"The following order of the President is published for the information and government of all concerned:—

EXECUTIVE MANSION, Washington, July 30.

"'It is the duty of every Government to give protection to its citizens, of whatever class, color, or condition, and especially to those wh are duly organized as soldiers in the public service. The law of nations, and the usages and customs of war, as carried on by civilized powers, permit no distinction as to color in the treatment of prisoners of war as public enemies. To sell or enslave any captured person on account of his color, is a relapse into barbarism, and a crime against the civilization of the age.

"'The Government of the United States will give the same protection to all its soldiers, and if the enemy shall sell or enslave any one because of his color, the offense shall be punished by retaliation upon the enemy's prisoners in our possession. It is, therefore, ordered, for every soldier of the United States, killed in violation of the laws of war, a rebel soldier shall be executed; and for every one enslaved by the enemy, or sold into slavery, a rebel soldier shall be placed at hard labor on the public works, and continued at such labor until the other shall be released and receive the treatment due to prisoners of war.

"'ABRAHAM LINCOLN.'"

"'By order of the Secretary of War.
"'E. D. TOWNSEND, Assistant Adjutant General.'"

That the President is in earnest the rebels soon began to find out, as witness the following order from his Secretary of War:

"WAR DEPARTMENT, Washington City, August 8, 1863.

"SIR: Your letter of the 3d inst., calling the attention of this Department to the cases of Orin H. Brown, William H. Johnston, and Wm. Wilson, three colored men captured on the gunboat Isaac Smith, has received consideration. This Department has directed that three rebel prisoners of South Carolina, if there be any such in our possession, and if not, three others, be confined in close custody and held as hostages for Brown, Johnston and Wilson, and that the fact be communicated to the rebel authorities at Richmond.

"Very respectfully your obedient servant,

"EDWIN M. STANTON, Secretary of War.

"The Hon. GIDEON WELLES, Secretary of the Navy."

And retaliation will be our practice now—man for man—to the bitter end.

LETTER OF CHARLES SUMNER,

Written with reference to the Convention held at Poughkeepsie, July 15th and 16th, 1863, to promote Colored Enlistments.

BOSTON, July 13th, 1863.

"I doubt if, in times past, our country could have expected from colored men any patriotic service. Such service is the return for protection. But now that protection has begun, the service should begin also. Nor should relative rights and duties be weighed with nicety. It is enough that our country, aroused at last to a sense of justice, seeks to enrol colored men among its defenders.

"If my counsels should reach such persons, I would say: enlist at once. Now is the day and now is the hour. Help to overcome your cruel enemies now battling against your country, and in this way you will surely overcome those other enemies hardly less cruel, here at home, who will still seek to degrade you. This is not the time to hesitate or to higgle. Do your duty to our country, and you will set an example of generous self-sacrifice which will conquer prejudice and open all hearts.

"Very faithfully yours,

"CHARLES SUMNER."

This recruitment poster issued by the War Department on July 21, 1863, called on African Americans to join the Union army.

An unidentified African-American soldier wearing the Union uniform stands for a portrait sometime between 1863 and 1865. Thousands of slaves risked severe punishment by leaving their plantations and joining the Union army.

When Slaves Ran Away

Slave owners were furious when they learned that many of their slaves had run away to join the Union army. They often punished the slaves' families. A slave in Missouri begged her husband to come home. She wrote that she had been beaten "most cruelly" with a leather strap because her husband had enlisted in the army.[3]

The Facts on Black Officers

★ Commissioned officers are lieutenants, captains, majors, colonels, and generals.

★ There were about eighty black commissioned officers by the end of the war. Among them were ministers and surgeons.

★ No African-American soldier reached a rank higher than captain. Nearly all troops were led by whites.

When Union soldiers came to Southern plantations, thousands of slaves risked punishment, and even death, by running away to become soldiers. The slave owners did not give up easily. Runaways who were caught were often beaten or shot dead. Two slaves had their left ears cut off when they were found trying to enlist. But for slaves, the chance to be free was worth any risk.

Elijah Marrs was a Kentucky slave who ran away to join the army. Twenty-seven other slaves went with him. In late September 1864, Marrs led the men to Louisville. They traveled at night, hiding in ditches to evade capture. At last, the men reached the army's recruiting office.

This photo, which was found in Cecil County, Maryland, shows an unidentified African-American Union soldier with his wife and two daughters. It is likely that the soldier belonged to a Maryland regiment. Runaway slaves joining the Union army could also be dangerous for the soldiers' families.

"I felt freedom in my bones," Marrs said. When he saw the American flag, all his fears disappeared.[4] Marrs became a sergeant in the Twelfth U.S. Colored Heavy Artillery.

Runaway slaves too young to fight were still able to help the Union army. After George Ellis escaped from slavery, he worked as a servant to an officer. In 1865, when Ellis was old enough to join the army, he joined the Fifty-fifth Massachusetts Colored Infantry.

It was not easy for a black man to become a soldier. Yet by the end of the war, one out of every eight soldiers in the Union army was African American.[5] For most, wearing the army uniform was a source of great pride.

"This was the biggest thing that ever happened in my life," said a former slave. "I felt like a man with a uniform on and a gun in my hand."[6]

During four years of war, nearly 100,000 blacks from the Confederate states joined the Union army. About 45,000 ex-slaves or freemen joined from the border states. Another 50,000 or more came from the Northern states and the Colorado Territory.

CHAPTER 4

THE FIRST REGIMENTS

Most white people had one big question: Would black men make good soldiers? The answer soon became clear.

"They are very much like white soldiers . . . and learn the drill quite as readily," said Thomas W. Higginson, the officer who led the First South Carolina Volunteers.[1]

After one terrible battle in Missouri, a newspaper reporter wrote, "It is useless to talk any more about Negro courage. The men fought like tigers, each and every one of them."[2]

The first all-black regiment in the Union Army was the First Louisiana Native Guards. The men showed their courage when they tried to capture Port Hudson, Louisiana, in May 1863.

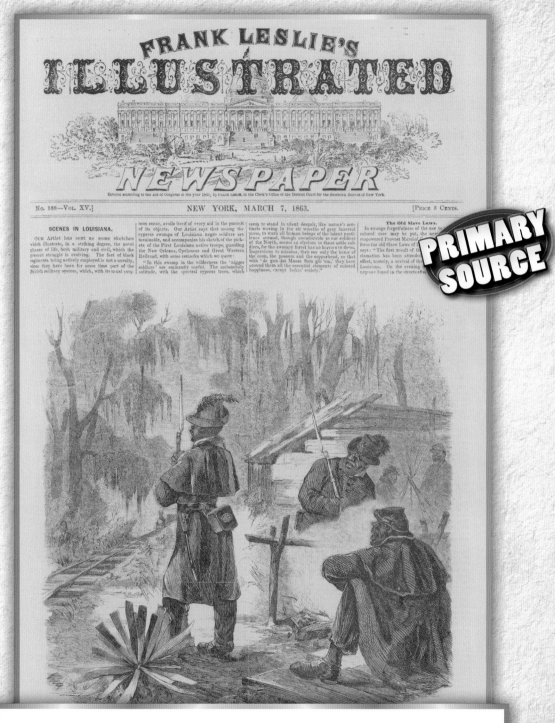

In this illustration from an issue of *Frank Leslie's Illustrated Newspaper* dated March 7, 1863, soldiers of the First Louisiana Native Guards stand watch at the Opelousas and Great Western Railroad in New Orleans.

One of the most famous all-black regiments, the Fifty-fourth Massachusetts, is shown in this mural depicting their courageous assault on Fort Wagner on Morris Island, South Carolina, in July 1863.

Unfairness to Black Soldiers

From the start, black soldiers were often treated badly in both the North and South. The black men in one Pennsylvania unit had stones thrown at them daily by soldiers in a white troop.[3]

The Native Guards pushed on through bullets and shells all day long. Even when soldiers were badly hurt, they went back to fighting as soon as they were bandaged. But the Confederates were fierce, and finally the Native Guards were forced to withdraw. Almost 300 African-American soldiers were dead, and more than 1,500 were badly wounded. Yet the men had proved that they were good soldiers.

The soldiers "fought like devils," wrote a white soldier from Wisconsin. "They made five charges on a battery that there was not the slightest chance of their taking, just . . . to show our boys that they *could* and *would* fight."[4]

Only a few days later, African-American soldiers showed their courage once again. At Milliken's Bend, Louisiana, a small force of white and black soldiers was attacked by 1,500 Confederates. The black soldiers had been drilled for only a few days. They had little idea of how to fight or how to use their weapons. Yet hundreds of them fought bravely and died in the hand-to-hand struggle.

"I have six broken bayonets to show how bravely my men fought," said Captain Matthew M. Miller, who lost half his Louisiana unit in the Union victory.[5]

✦✦✦✦✦

It is easy to understand why African Americans would fight for the North. Yet there were also some African Americans who joined the Confederate army. Why would black men want to fight for the South?

Not all blacks in the South were slaves. Some were free men who owned property. They were afraid it would be taken away by Union soldiers, and so they stayed loyal to the South. Also, many slaves were frightened by stories that Northerners would treat them far worse than Southerners.[6]

Many blacks were forced to work in the Confederate army. They cooked food, carried wounded soldiers on stretchers, and

During the Civil War, about 30,000 African Americans served in the Union navy. This portrait shows an African-American sailor in uniform.

built roads. The Confederate army needed more soldiers, too. Some—but not all—Southerners thought that black men should fight. "He [the black man] must play an important part in this war," said a Louisiana farmer. "He *caused* the fight."[7]

But by the time Confederate leaders finally agreed to enlist African Americans, the war was almost over. Few slaves joined the Confederate army.

African Americans also served bravely at sea. In the North, about 30,000 African Americans served in the U.S. Navy. This was about one-fourth of all Union sailors.[8]

One of the most famous seamen was Robert Smalls, a South Carolina slave. Smalls became a pilot on the Confederate ship *Planter*. One evening, the crew was alone on the steamship. Smalls planned a daring escape. He quickly put on the captain's uniform. Then he carefully guided the ship out of Charleston Harbor, past the Confederate troops on the shore. He steamed over to a Union ship and offered them his boat. The *Planter* became a Union ship, with Smalls as its pilot. He served as pilot of the *Planter*, as well as other boats, for the rest of the war.

CHAPTER 5

★

SEPARATE BUT UNEQUAL

African Americans fought bravely and were praised for their courage during the Civil War. But they were not treated as equals to whites. Their days were often filled with hard jobs known as fatigue duty. They dug trenches, built roads, and unloaded supplies. Black soldiers were not able to devote their time to drilling and preparing for battle. "Instead of the musket, it is the spade and wheelbarrow and the axe," complained one soldier in a Louisiana unit.[1]

Some soldiers became angry, saying they were still being treated like slaves. Private William G. Barcroft refused to work one day. He said he was being used as a laborer, not a soldier.

Barcroft was punished for not obeying an officer. He was sentenced to two years in an army prison.

The white soldiers drilled, headed off to battle, or rested in camp. Meanwhile, the black soldiers often worked eight to ten hours a day doing hard labor. As a result, the black soldiers were tired and poorly prepared for combat. They had worn-out uniforms and dirty guns. It is not surprising that their spirits were often low.

The officers complained until the War Department finally took action. In June 1864, a new rule said that black soldiers must not be given more fatigue duty than white soldiers. Still, this rule was often ignored.

Soldier Deaths

Twice as many African-American soldiers died from disease during the war as whites. The blacks had worn-out clothing, so they suffered more in bad weather. Also, many white doctors did not want to take care of black soldiers.[2]

This September 1864 photo taken in Petersburg, Virginia, shows the Thirty-ninth U.S. Colored Infantry. The white field officers pose in front, and the black soldiers had to stand in the background. The photo serves as a symbol of the unequal treatment black soldiers faced while fighting in the Union army throughout the war.

Money was another sore point. White soldiers received $13 each month, plus extra money for clothing. Blacks were given only $10 per month, and $3 was subtracted for their clothing. This left the black soldier with only $7. That was about half the pay a white soldier received.

The 5,000 black soldiers recruited by the War Department had been promised the same pay and rations as other soldiers in the

Union army. When they found out that whites were getting more, black soldiers were furious. "It is a shame the way they treat us," said London S. Langley, a soldier in the Fifty-fourth Massachusetts Infantry (Colored). "Our officers tell me now that we are soldiers. . . . If we were, we would get the same pay as the white men."[3]

Many black soldiers refused to accept their $10 paychecks. The men of the Massachusetts Fifty-fourth and Fifty-fifth said they would take no pay at all if it was less than the amount being given to white soldiers. It was not until June 1864 that the government provided equal pay for the U.S. Colored Troops.

Black soldiers were also given harsher punishments if they were captured by the enemy. Confederates claimed they would treat captured soldiers as runaway slaves. Their officers would be executed.

One of the most brutal battles took place at Fort Pillow in Tennessee. Fifteen hundred Confederate troops attacked the fort in April 1864. It was held by 570 Union soldiers—half of them black. The Union soldiers were finally forced to drop their guns. Many raised their hands in the air to surrender. Yet the

The brutal massacre at Fort Pillow is shown in this illustration. Many African-American soldiers were killed during the battle. "Remember Fort Pillow" became a rallying cry for African Americans during the war.

Confederates savagely shot down the Union soldiers. The killings spurred on blacks through the rest of the war with the battle cry, "Remember Fort Pillow!"

During the four years of the Civil War, African-American soldiers faced many injustices—less money, shabby uniforms, poor equipment, and the risk of being shot or enslaved if they were captured. Yet they fought with courage and loyalty.

The war ended in 1865. More than 180,000 African Americans had served in the Northern army and navy. Before the war, more than half of these men had been slaves in the South.[4]

Most African Americans went home after the war. In the North, many soldiers used the money they had earned to buy land or to get training in a skill, such as bricklaying. In the South, many African Americans became field workers on or near the plantations where they had been slaves.[5] Their lives were not much different than they were before the war. But now they were

Equal Rights

Laws were passed to make sure African Americans were treated more fairly. In 1865, the Thirteenth Amendment to the U.S. Constitution put an end to slavery throughout the United States. Three years later, the Fourteenth Amendment gave African-American citizens equal protection under the law and the right to hold a political office. In 1870, the Fifteenth Amendment gave African-American men the right to vote.

Congress of the United States of America;

At the __second__ Session,

Begun and held at the City of Washington, on Monday, the __fifth__ day of December, one thousand eight hundred and sixty-__four__

A RESOLUTION

Submitting to the legislatures of the several States a proposition to amend the Constitution of the United States.

Resolved by the Senate and House of Representatives of the United States of America in Congress assembled, (two-thirds of both houses concurring), that the following article be proposed to the legislatures of the several States as an amendment to the Constitution of the United States, which, when ratified by three-fourths of said legislatures, shall be valid, to all intents and purposes, as a part of the said Constitution, namely: Article XIII. Section 1. Neither slavery nor involuntary servitude, except as a punishment for crime whereof the party shall have been duly convicted, shall exist within the United States, or any place subject to their jurisdiction. Section 2. Congress shall have power to enforce this article by appropriate legislation.

Schuyler Colfax
Speaker of the House of Representatives.

H. Hamlin
Vice President of the United States
and President of the Senate.

Approved February 1. 1865.

Abraham Lincoln

The Thirteenth Amendment to the Constitution, approved by Congress in January 1865, abolished slavery in the United States. President Lincoln signed this copy of the amendment.

In this photo, an African-American sharecropper plows a field in Virginia. After the war, many African Americans returned to the South, where they worked as sharecroppers. Although slavery had ended, it would be a long and difficult struggle for African Americans to achieve equal rights.

sharecroppers, not slaves. They farmed the land in exchange for part of the money the crop would make at the market.

The war had ended, but the fight for equal rights for all Americans was just beginning. African Americans had little money or education. Life was not easy for them. Over the next hundred years, they would struggle to be treated as equal citizens.

"If we hadn't become soldiers, all might have gone back as it was before," said Thomas Long, a former slave who joined the First South Carolina Volunteers. "But now things can never go back, because we have showed our energy and our courage."[6]

TIMELINE

1619

August: First African slaves are sold in Jamestown, Virginia.

1793

The cotton gin is invented, giving new life to the slave industry in the South.

1860

November: Abraham Lincoln is elected president.

December: South Carolina is the first of eleven states to secede from the Union.

1861

February: Confederate States of America is formed.

April 12: Fort Sumter is attacked; the Civil War begins.

July 21: Confederacy wins the First Battle of Bull Run.

1862

May 12: Robert Smalls makes a daring escape from the Confederacy with the steamship *Planter*.

July 17: Congress rules that black Americans can now enlist in the Union army.

August: The War Department organizes 5,000 black volunteers to fight in the Union army.

September: Louisiana Native Guards becomes first all-black regiment to formally join Union army.

1863

January 1: Lincoln issues the Emancipation Proclamation.

May 27: Native Guards attack Port Hudson, Louisiana.

July 18: The Fifty-fourth Massachusetts Regiment leads an assault on Fort Wagner, South Carolina.

1864

April: Black soldiers are ruthlessly shot down by Confederates at Fort Pillow, Tennessee.

June 15: Congress grants equal pay for black soldiers.

September 29: Black soldiers fight heroically at Battle of New Market Heights, Virginia. Fourteen earn the Medal of Honor.

October 2: About 600 black soldiers of the Fifth and Sixth U.S. Colored Cavalry attack the salt furnaces at Saltville, Virginia (First Battle of Saltville).

1865

March 23: Confederacy issues law to use slaves as soldiers.

April 9: Confederate general Robert E. Lee surrenders to Union general Ulysses S. Grant.

April 15: Lincoln dies after being shot; Andrew Johnson becomes president.

May 13: The last battle of the Civil War is fought at Palmetto Ranch, Texas.

December 6: The Thirteenth Amendment to the Constitution abolishes slavery in the United States.

CHAPTER NOTES

CHAPTER 1. A NEW COUNTRY

1. Russell Duncan, *Where Death and Glory Meet: Robert Gould Shaw and the 54th Massachusetts Infantry* (Athens, Ga.: University of Georgia Press, 1999), p. 112.
2. Ervin L. Jordan, Jr., *Black Confederates and Afro-Yankees in Civil War Virginia* (Charlottesville: University Press of Virginia, 1995), p. 272.
3. Catherine Clinton, *The Black Soldier* (Boston: Houghton Mifflin, 2000), pp. 22–23.
4. Geoffrey C. Ward, *The Civil War: An Illustrated History* (New York: Alfred A. Knopf, 1990), p. 12.
5. African-American Civil War Soldiers, Frederick Douglass, n.d., <http://americancivilwar.com/colored/frederick_douglass/html> (June 27, 2003).
6. Dudley Taylor Cornish, *The Sable Arm: Negro Troops in the Union Army, 1861–1865* (New York: W. W. Norton, 1966), p. 5.

CHAPTER 2. THE WAY IS BARRED

1. Noah Andre Trudeau, *Like Men of War: Black Troops in the Civil War, 1862–1865* (Boston: Little, Brown and Co., 1998), p. 179.
2. Catherine Clinton, *The Black Soldier* (Boston: Houghton Mifflin, 2000), p. 23.
3. Charles H. Wesley, *Negro Americans in the Civil War: From Slavery to Citizenship* (New York: Publishers Company, Inc., 1967), p. 147.

CHAPTER 3. RECRUITMENT

1. Joseph T. Glatthaar, *Forged in Battle: The Civil War Alliance of Black Soldiers and White Officers* (New York: Penguin Books, 1990), p. 3.
2. Ibid., p. 74.
3. Ibid., p. 70.
4. "Recruitment and Training Center," Camp Nelson, Kentucky, n.d., <http://www.campnelson.org/history/recruitment.htm> (June 27, 2003).
5. Hondon B. Hargrove, *Black Union Soldiers in the Civil War* (Jefferson, N.C.: McFarland & Company, 1988), p. 207.
6. Glatthaar, p. 79.

CHAPTER 4. THE FIRST REGIMENTS

1. Christopher Looby, editor, *The Complete Civil War Journal and Selected Letters of Thomas Wentworth Higginson* (Chicago: University of Chicago Press, 2000), p. 249.
2. Dudley Taylor Cornish, *The Sable Arm: Negro Troops in the Union Army, 1861–1865* (New York: W. W. Norton, 1966) p. 77.
3. Joseph T. Glatthaar, *Forged in Battle: The Civil War Alliance of Black Soldiers and White Officers* (New York: Penguin Books, 1990), p. 196.
4. Noah Andre Trudeau, *Like Men of War: Black Troops in the Civil War, 1862–1865* (Boston: Little, Brown and Co., 1998), p. 44.
5. Hondon B. Hargrove, *Black Union Soldiers in the Civil War* (Jefferson, N.C.: McFarland & Company, 1988), p. 146.
6. Shelby Foote, *The Civil War: A Narrative, From Red River to Appomattox* (New York: Random House, 1974), p. 753.
7. Geoffrey C. Ward, *The Civil War: An Illustrated History* (New York: Alfred A. Knopf, 1990), p. 253.
8. Charles H. Wesley, *Negro Americans in the Civil War: From Slavery to Citizenship* (New York: Publishers Company, Inc., 1967), p. 167.

CHAPTER 5. SEPARATE BUT UNEQUAL

1. Joseph T. Glatthaar, *Forged in Battle: The Civil War Alliance of Black Soldiers and White Officers* (New York: Penguin Books, 1990), p. 183.
2. Geoffrey C. Ward, *The Civil War: An Illustrated History* (New York: Alfred A. Knopf, Inc., 1990), p. 252.
3. Noah Andre Trudeau, *Like Men of War: Black Troops in the Civil War, 1862–1865* (New York: Little, Brown, and Company, 1998), p. 253.
4. Versalle F. Washington, *Eagles on Their Buttons: A Black Infantry Regiment in the Civil War* (Columbia, Missouri: University of Missouri Press, 1999), p. x.
5. Trudeau, p. 463.
6. Edited by Steven Mintz, "Excerpts from Slave Narratives," University of Houston, n.d., <http://vi.uh.edu/pages/mintz/38.htm> (June 27, 2003).

GLOSSARY

bayonet—A steel blade attached at the end of a rifle.

border states—States that allowed slavery, yet were part of the Union: Maryland, Delaware, Kansas, and Missouri.

civil war—A war between people of the same country.

colored/Negro—Words that were used for African Americans.

Confederate States of America—The new country formed in 1861 by the eleven Southern states that withdrew from the United States: South Carolina, Mississippi, Florida, Alabama, Georgia, Louisiana, Texas, Virginia, Arkansas, North Carolina, and Tennessee. Also called the Confederacy.

contraband—A slave who escaped during the Civil War and took refuge with the Union army.

Emancipation Proclamation—Abraham Lincoln's document that declared slaves in the rebelling states to be free.

enlist—To enroll in the armed forces.

plantation—A large farm.

ration—A set amount of food.

recruit—To enroll people as members of the armed forces.

secede—To withdraw or break away.

FURTHER READING

Books

Allen, Thomas B. *Harriet Tubman, Secret Agent: How Daring Slaves and Free Blacks Spied for the Union During the Civil War.* Washington, D.C.: National Geographic, 2009.

Claus, J. Matteson. *Life on a Civil War Battlefield.* New York: Crabtree Publishing Company, 2011.

Haskins, Jim. *Black, Blue & Gray: African Americans in the Civil War.* New York: Simon & Schuster Books for Young Readers, 1998.

Reis, Ronald A. *African Americans and the Civil War.* New York: Chelsea House Publishers, 2009.

Roche, Tim. *Soldiers of the Civil War.* Chicago: Heinemann Library, 2011.

Internet Addresses

African American Odyssey: The Civil War
<http://memory.loc.gov/ammem/aaohtml/exhibit/aopart4.html>

Africans in America: The Civil War
<http://www.pbs.org/wgbh/aia/part4/4narr5.html>

INDEX